A VITAL SIMPLICITY

Charles Wagner's 'The Simple Life' revisited

by Suzanne Searcy Johnson

with excerpts by Charles Wagner

1st Edition
ISBN: 978-0-9837183-4-5

suzannesjohnson.com

*for my brother and sisters
who ground me*

~

A book should be luminous but not voluminous
- Christian Nestell Bovee

~

Contents

Introduction

I have felt the pull of simplicity (and danced around minimalism) for decades. It began in 1995 when I got my hands on the book "Simplify Your Life: 100 Ways to Slow Down and Enjoy the Things that Really Matter" by Elaine St. James. Even then, I was able to see the complications in my everyday life. I read this book faithfully every January for years attempting to reset with my new year's resolutions. However, there was nothing solid to tether me to lasting change.

Then, about 10 years ago, I discovered Charles Wagner's "The Simple Life". Though originally published in 1895, it could have been describing life in the 21st century. And Wagner's words filled a gap for me. He provided a path to an internal change that drives action. Once my mission is clearly defined, my actions naturally follow. And the excess that clutters my mind and my life falls away.

After discovering the work was public domain, I wanted to re-publish it but didn't have a clear vision of how to make it fresh for today's audience. It wasn't until recently that the concept of infusing Wagner's words with my poetry came into focus. The message is deep and rich, and poetry has a way of communicating concepts in a few words and images.

I have replaced some words with synonyms and paraphrased to enhance readability for today's audience while attempting to honor the beautiful language of the writer. In the spirit of simplicity, I have chosen only portions (approximately 20% of the original text) to include in this book. Each chapter includes poems, selections from "The Simple Life" (set apart by italics), and my own commentary. Finally, an infographic is provided at the end of the book that condenses this content further by including only main points.

My hope is to bring Wagner's insights to new readers and breathe fresh life into his words by curating the original manuscript content and adding a layer of interpretation through poetry.

Preface by Charles Wagner

The sick man, wasted by fever, consumed with thirst, dreams in his sleep of a fresh stream wherein he bathes, or of a clear fountain from which he drinks in great draughts. So, amid the confused restlessness of modern life, our wearied minds dream of simplicity.

Simplicity does not belong to economic or social phases; rather, it is a spirit, able to vivify and modify lives of very different sorts. Far from being reduced to vainly regretting it, we may, I affirm, make it the object of resolve, the end of practical effort.

Aspire to simple living? That means, aspire to fulfil the highest human destiny. All of men's agitations for greater justice and more light have been also movements toward a simpler life; and the simplicity of olden times, in manners, art, and ideas, still keeps its incomparable value, only because it achieved the setting forth in high relief of certain essential sentiments and certain permanent truths. It is a simplicity to cherish and reverence; but he little comprehends it who thinks its peculiar virtue lies in its outward manifestations. In brief, **if it is impossible for us to be simple in the forms our fathers used, we may remain simple, or return to simplicity, in their spirit. Our ways are not their ways, but the journey's end remains in truth the same.** It is always the polestar that guides the seaman, whether he cruise under sail or on a steamship. To make headway toward this end, with the means at our command, that is the essential thing, today as yesterday; and it is by frequent deviations from our route, that we have confused and complicated our life.

Should I succeed in making others share this quite spiritual notion of simplicity, I shall not have labored in vain. Too many hampering futilities separate us from that ideal of the true, the just, and the good, that should warm and animate our hearts. All this brushwood, under pretext of sheltering us and our happiness, has ended by shutting out our sun. When shall we have the courage to meet the delusive temptations of our complex and unprofitable life with the sage's challenge: "Out of my light"?*

Paris, May 1895

*refers to Diogenes' words to Alexander the Great in 336 BC to "stand a little out of my sun"

1 | Complication

We suffer the consequences of a too-artificial life.

Dandelion

Dandelion
Waves in the
Wind
Breeze catches
Seeds
Scatters them
Up and
Out and
Away

Mind
Moves through the
Haze
Chases random
Thoughts
Follows the
Posts and
Clicks and
Ideas

Focus
Vanishes in the
Clutter
Hitches a
Ride on those
Seeds
Adrift and
Absent and
Lost

"From the cradle to the grave, in his needs as in his pleasures, in his conception of the world and of himself, the man of modern times struggles through a maze of endless complication. Nothing is simple any longer: neither thought nor action; not pleasure, not even dying. I believe that thousands of our fellow-men, suffering the consequences of a too-artificial life, will be grateful if we try to give expression to their discontent, and to justify the regret for naturalness which vaguely oppresses them."

Wagner's picture of the discontented soul, encumbered by distractions and pretention, speaks as effectively to society in the 21st century as it did when he put pen to paper 125 years ago. The phrases "too-artificial life" and "regret for naturalness" scream the truth of numerous societies in many times: slowing down and experiencing true connection with our fellow human beings, with God, and with nature can be an uphill climb while we are entranced by things and striving to attain rather than simply to be.

"Do not say that we live in more trying times than our ancestors, for things seen from afar are often seen imperfectly: it is moreover scarcely gracious to complain of not having been born in the days of one's grandfather. From the beginning of the world it has been hard to see clearly; right thinking has been difficult everywhere and always."

We are reminded that the need for simplicity is nothing new. Every generation laments the loss of the "good old days". And we continually return to certain truths.

Lamp

I have a
Lamp
It rests on my
Table
Prominently on
Display
Gilded edges and
Vibrant colors
But no
Light

The bulb
Itself is
Blackened
Obscured by
Dirt and
Muck and
Filth
But the
Lampshade is
Lovely

I'll leave it
As is
With no
Illumination
No matter
I can
Sit in the
Dark

Pretend I can
See

Perhaps there is
Another option
Free the
Glow from what
Blocks it
And let the
Radiance
Once again
Light my
Way

"We must search out, set free, restore to honor the true life, assign things to their proper places, and remember that the center of human progress is moral growth. What is a good lamp? It is not the most elaborate, the finest wrought, that of the most precious metal. A good lamp is a lamp that gives good light. And so also we are men and citizens, not by reason of the number of our goods and the pleasures we procure for ourselves, not through our intellectual and artistic culture, nor because of the honors and independence we enjoy; but by virtue of the strength of our moral fiber. And this is not a truth of to-day but a truth of all times.

"When one reviews the individual causes that disturb and complicate our social life, they all lead back to one general cause, which is this: **the confusion of the secondary with the essential**. *Material comfort, education, liberty, the whole of civilization--these things constitute the frame of the*

picture; but the frame no more makes the picture than the frock the monk or the uniform the soldier. Here the picture is man, and man with his most intimate possessions--namely, his conscience, his character, and his will. And while we have been elaborating and garnishing the frame, we have forgotten, neglected, disfigured the picture. Thus are we loaded with external good, and miserable in spiritual life. And when the depth of our being is stirred, with its need of loving, aspiring, fulfilling its destiny, it feels the anguish of one buried alive--is smothered under the mass of secondary things that weigh it down and deprive it of light and air."

This analogy of the picture and the frame illustrates that if the energy we spend on the external robs us of building character and self-control, our souls are deprived of what they need to flourish. A spiritual life that is choked out by distractions can leave us isolated and depressed.

Social media – one of the chief distractions today which is discussed again in chapter 4 – provides the illusion of connectedness. However, it often results in parasocial - relationships, in which we feel a false sense of closeness with others through technology but are not actually connected in real life.

It's a balancing act...this utilizing technology and modern conveniences while at the same time breathing in the beauty that is pure silence and our natural environment. But this balance is a worthy goal. Totally shunning one or the other leaves us isolated when we were created to participate in life and with humanity.

| Balance

Burdens

I started down this
Path
Backpack filled with
Necessities
And "just in case"
Objects
Unaware of the
Weight

I climbed the craggy
Rocks
Holding to a steady
Stick
But then I
Tripped
Pulled down by the
Burden

It occurred to
Me
Let go of the
Unessential
And I removed one
Item
And made my way
Further

Came upon a
Waterfall
Waded joyfully in the

Creek
Until my feet
Slipped
And all was
Soaked

Removing ruined
Belongings
I found there was no
Need
No grip on
Things
Required in this
Journey

So I left all
There
On the verdant
Ground
And in the open
Sky
And walked
Unencumbered
To my bright
Destiny

"At no epoch have the exterior conditions which man has made for himself by his industry or his knowledge, been able to exempt him from care for the state of his inner life.

"And whatever be his road, to make toward his goal, the traveler must not lose himself in crossways, nor hamper his

movements with useless burdens. Let him heed well his direction
and forces, and keep good faith; and that he may the better
devote himself to the essential, let him simplify his baggage."

Wagner makes the point that we must care for the state of
our inner lives, regardless of external circumstances. By
removing "useless burdens", we're able to progress
towards whatever personal goals fall in line with our
individual purpose.

So how do we eliminate the unessential and find balance?
The change must be come from within. The following
chapters will present areas in which we've allowed
complication to infiltrate our lives and our society. It will
offer solutions in broad strokes coupled with clear, specific
actions we can take to focus on the essential. Finally,
promises for enhanced lives will be offered. Just as
cluttered minds and lives are nothing new, simplicity itself
remains a guiding light, whether 100 years ago, today, or
100 years in the future.

2 | Wants

As an inevitable consequence of the law that needs are increased by their satisfaction, the more goods a man has, the more he wants.

Hunger

Hunger
Overtakes me
I must have
Food
To fill and
Sustain

So I eat
Bread and
Meat and
Fruit
And I am
Filled
Just for a
Moment

Then the
Familiar craving
Comes
I want
More
So I
Take
Consume and
Devour
Until I am
Satiated

But it never
Lasts
Even while I
Sit

Taste of my
Previous meal
Still on my
Lips
Once again
Hunger
Overtakes me

"Could our fathers have foreseen that we should someday have at our disposal the means and forces we now use in sustaining and defending our material life, they would have predicted for us an increase of independence, and therefore of happiness, and a decrease in competition for worldly goods: they might even have thought that through the simplification of life thus made possible, a higher degree of morality would be attained. None of these things has come to pass. Neither happiness, nor brotherly love, nor power for good has been increased."

What was true in 1900 is especially accurate today. The advancements we've seen in the last 25 years alone are nothing short of miraculous. Our phones allow us access to more information, greater opportunities to connect, interactive maps to get us places, and vast entertainment. And yet we waste more time and become more isolated and divided than ever.

"Upward from a certain income, fee, or salary, life becomes possible: below that it is impossible. You must be without a penny, if only for a day or two, and try to live in this world of ours, to have any idea of the needs of him whose purse is empty."

It's important to note that Wagner acknowledges the need for a living wage. The material needs vs. wants discussion is irrelevant for those who do not have their basic needs met.

"The complexity of our life appears in the number of our material needs. What material things does a man need to live under the best conditions? A healthy diet, simple clothing, a sanitary dwelling-place, air and exercise.

"Never has the question of food and shelter been sharper or more absorbing than since we are better nourished, better clothed, and better housed than ever.

"Among those in easy circumstances and the rich, are too many people who forget that what they possess could serve a better purpose than procuring pleasure for themselves, only to find in the end that one never has enough. Our needs, in place of the servants that they should be, have become a turbulent and seditious crowd, a legion of tyrants in miniature. A man enslaved to his needs may best be compared to a bear with a ring in its nose, that is led about and made to dance at will.

Rather than freeing us to care for one another, our possessions – if not put in their right place – can own us. We are like dogs chasing our tails in pursuit of acquisition. If we will just stop, we will realize we have enough to share.

"He is senseless who seeks for happiness in material prosperity alone. **Do not confound what you possess with what you are.**

"An animal is satisfied when it has eaten; it lies down and sleeps. A man also can lie down and sleep for a time, but it never lasts. When he becomes accustomed to this contentment, he tires of it and demands a greater. Man's appetite is not appeased by food; it increases with eating."

This disturbing paradox is real. In the absence of actions to counter complacency, we become dissatisfied with the abundance around us and crave still more. The cycle continues.

And there is another paradox: that of choice. One of the first studies that pointed to the adverse effects of choice was the "Jam Study" (Iyengar and Lepper). Researchers found that more people purchased jam when fewer options were available. And we are a society mired in options. Walk down a grocery store aisle sometime if you doubt this. Currently, Arizona Iced Tea offers 14 different flavors, Cheerios 16, Pringles 34…you get the picture. Do we really need all these options? Or does greater choice potentially lead to greater dissatisfaction?

| Conflict

Jealousy

She has what I
Want
It's really that
Simple
Fancy clothes and
Lovely smile and
Perfect, angelic
Children

Her home is
Adorned with
Tasteful and
Quite exquisite
Furniture
I'm afraid to
Sit on the pristine
Sofa

I would take it
From her if I
Could
Steal her perfect
Life
Her precious
Possessions
Because I need to feel
Whole

How silly
When I have
More than I

Need
And most of what I
Want
That I would
Take
Instead of opening my
Hands

When will I
Learn?
Her success does not
Diminish
My own
And lifting her
Up
Elevates me in the
Process

"If we have not become happier, neither have we grown more peaceful and fraternal. The more desires and needs a man has, the more occasion he finds for conflict with his fellow-men; and these conflicts are more bitter in proportion as their causes are less just. It is the law of nature to fight for bread, for the necessities. Quite different is the battle for the superfluous--for ambition, privilege, inclination, luxury. Never has hunger driven man to such baseness as have envy, avarice, and thirst for pleasure. Egotism grows more maleficent as it becomes more refined. We of these times have seen an increase of hostile feeling among brothers, and our hearts are less at peace than ever.

"It is true that in the fierce struggle for possession, we come to hate those who possess, and to deny the right of property when

this right is in the hands of others and not in our own. But the bitterness of attack against others' possessions is only a new proof of the extraordinary importance we attach to possession itself."

Jealousy is at the core of what Wagner describes here. You have what I want, so I must fight and climb and grab what I can rather than open my eyes to the abundance that already exists around me. At a corporate level, there is a constant drive for market share. While this is not in and of itself a bad thing, the idea that the pie is only so big permeates all of our lives, not just corporate America. Somehow, we've missed the idea that another person's success doesn't have to diminish our own. The pie can grow larger.

Tightrope

I walk the
Tightrope
Long, weighted
Pole in my
Hands
Holding perpendicular
To my
Frame
Keeping me in
Balance

There is a burden
On the stick's
End
Pulling me
Slightly to the
Left
It is material
Prosperity
A noble and worthy
Goal
But will it make me
Fall?

There is an offset
On the other
End
Raising my body
Slowly to the
Right
It is a spiritual

Connectedness
To the earth
And the heavens
And to
Others

Somehow in the
Middle of this
World and
Wire
I've found my
Equilibrium
In thoughts of
Myself
And a heart for
Others
And I am now
Steady

"Someone objects: 'Then you make wholesale condemnation of progress, and would lead us back to the good old times--to retire from the world perhaps.'

"Not at all. The desire to resuscitate the past is the most unfruitful and dangerous of Utopian dreams, and the art of good living does not consist in retiring from life. But we are trying to throw light upon one of the errors that drag most heavily upon human progress, in order to find a remedy for it-- namely, the belief that man becomes happier and better by the increase of outward well-being. Nothing is falser than this pretended social axiom; on the contrary, that material prosperity without an offset, diminishes the capacity for happiness and

debases character, is a fact which a thousand examples are at hand to prove. The worth of a civilization is the worth of the man at its center. When this man lacks moral rectitude, progress only makes bad worse, and further embroils social problems."

Throughout the book, Wagner identifies the "offset" of material prosperity as morality. However, this isn't a religious morality. Rather he describes a morality in relation to others – a conscious belief that a person's self-worth and even happiness is dependent upon his or recognition of our dependence upon each other.

Craving

Sweet taste
On my waiting
Tongue
Rich chocolate
With a slight
Hint of
Sugar
Delicious and
Deep and
Delectable
And it should be
Enough

But it only
Awakens
Inside me a
Craving
One bite merely
Reminds me
How much I want
More
Intensifies
Instead of
Satisfying

No need to hold
Back
I will give in to
This pressing
Need
One more tasty
Bite

And then yet
Another
Wants merging with
Needs
Until I
Surrender

"Money will not answer for everything: it is a power, but it is not all-powerful. Nothing complicates life, demoralizes man, perverts the normal course of society like being overly motivated by money. Wherever it reigns, everybody is duped by everybody else: one can no longer put trust in persons or things, no longer obtain anything of value. We would not be detractors of money, but this general law must be applied to it: **Everything in its own place***. When gold, which should be a servant, becomes a tyrannical power, affronting morality, dignity and liberty, it is time to rise against this gross and criminal delusion. The most precious things that man possesses he has almost always received gratuitously: let him learn so to give them.*

"How dangerous it is to accustom your sons and daughters to a style of living beyond your means and theirs! In the first place, it is very bad for your purse; in the second place it develops a contemptuous spirit in the very bosom of the family.

"Let your needs rule you, pamper them--you will see them multiply like insects in the sun. The more you give them, the more they demand."

And here is the key, a subtle, tiny phrase: "Let your needs rule you, pamper them." This is the line that differentiates normal life and enjoyment of material goods from constant grabbing, reaching for more. And he alludes to the dangers of living above our means in that it teaches our children to value material possessions too highly.

There is also a recognition that most precious things in life are given freely. It follows that abundance in life is found as we learn to give.

3 | Pleasure

The more costly toys a child has, the more feasts and curious entertainments, the less is he amused.

| # Discontent

Blocks

Child plays
Hour after hour
Stacking blocks
Knocking down
Holding wooden
Cubes in his
Tender hands
He is
Entertained

Leave the
Floor bare
Except for
These sturdy
Pieces
He finds his
Way
His interest is
Held

Add Legos
To the mix
And coloring
Books
Trains and trucks
And why not
Screens?
He soon becomes
Bored

Let his
Amusement
Be in the
Simple things
Let his
Vision sharpen on
One thing at a
Time
Cut through the
Clutter
And find
Joy

"Let us be temperate in our methods of entertaining youth, and especially let us not thoughtlessly create for them artificial needs.

"If you wish to train your children for liberty, bring them up simply, and do not for a moment fear that in so doing you are putting obstacles in the way of their happiness. It will be quite the contrary. The more costly toys a child has, the more feasts and curious entertainments, the less is he amused."

This revelation by Wagner is backed up by research. A study from the University of Toledo in Ohio suggests "an abundance of toys present reduced quality of toddlers' play." Having fewer toys can lead a young child to focus and engage in more creative, imaginative play. (Dauch, Imwalle and Ocasio) The study, "The influence of the number of toys in the environment on toddlers' play", wss published in the journal *Infant Behavior and Development.* Fewer toys, it turns out, result in healthier play, and, ultimately, deeper cognitive development.

As parents, sometimes it's much easier to entertain our children with electronics. Letting them spend hours on their phones and playing video games might actually teach our children to take the easy road, to be spoon-fed entertainment, and to miss out on the abundance of the world around us.

"From morning till night, wherever we go, the people we meet are hurried, worried, preoccupied. Some have spilt their good blood in the miserable conflicts of petty politics: others are disheartened by the meanness and jealousy they have encountered in the world of literature or art. Commercial competition troubles the sleep of not a few. The working classes suffer the consequences of a ceaseless industrial struggle. It is becoming disagreeable to govern, because authority is diminishing; to teach, because respect is vanishing. Wherever one turns there is matter for discontent."

Wagner enumerates sources of discontent – particularly relevant today. Politics, commercial competition, lack of respect all take a toll on the individual spirit and collective community.

"Joy is not in things, it is in us, and I hold to the belief that the causes of our present unrest, of this contagious discontent spreading everywhere, are in us at least as much as in exterior conditions.

"To give oneself up heartily to diversion one must feel himself on a solid basis, must believe in life and find it within him. And here lies our weakness. So many of us are at variance with life. How do you think a man can be amused while he has his doubts whether after all life is worth living? Excess of all kinds has blurred our senses and poisoned our faculty for happiness.

Deeply attainted at its root, the desire to live, persistent in spite of everything, seeks satisfaction in cheats and baubles.

"We must not confound pleasure with the instruments of pleasure. To be a painter, does it suffice to arm one's self with a brush, or does the purchase at great cost of a Stradivarius make one a musician? But with a bit of crayon a great artist makes an immortal sketch. It needs talent or genius to paint; and to amuse one's self, the faculty of being happy: whoever possesses it is amused at slight cost. This faculty is destroyed by skepticism, artificial living, over-abuse; it is fostered by confidence, moderation and normal habits of thought and action."

Here a link between continual pleasure-seeking and depression is presented. Seeking satisfaction from external sources rather than finding internal joy leads to disappointment and restlessness. His formula for internal joy includes "confidence, moderation, and normal habits of thought and action." Perhaps this isn't exciting, but it is a spiritual principle nonetheless: Discipline and moderate living contribute to overall contentment and happiness.

| Diversions

Innocence

I was once
Innocent
Ran freely through
Meadows
Bare feet
Tickled by
Flowers
Daisy chains and
Four-leaf
Clovers my
Diversions

But the
Land of my
Amusement
Is becoming
Barren
Choked out by
Weeds of
Numbing
I choose
Artificial ease and
Comfort

I'm losing my
Way
Forfeiting precious
Joy
Trading freedom for
Illusions of

Relief
I've had
Enough

Shoes and
Socks come
Off
Toes wiggle in
Dew-tipped
Grass
Sun heats my
Freckled forearms
And delight begins
Anew

"Unhappily, innocence is disappearing. The mind, warped by alcohol, by the passion for gambling, and by unhealthy literature, contracts little by little perverted tastes. Artificial life makes eruption into communities once simple in their pleasures, and it is like destructive insects to the vine. The robust tree of rustic joy finds its sap drained, its leaves turning yellow.

"Pleasure and money: people take them for the two wings of the same bird! A gross illusion! **Pleasure, like all other truly precious things in this world, cannot be bought or sold.** *If you wish to be amused, you must do your part toward it; that is the essential. Pleasure and simplicity are two old acquaintances. Entertain simply, meet your friends simply. If you come from work well done, are as amiable and genuine as possible toward your companions, and speak no evil of the absent, your success is sure."*

There is a societal pull to opt for numbing distractions over genuine feeling. But life is much, much richer when lived fully. Wagner's simple formula: Be dutiful in work, genuine with companions, and avoid gossip. Live simply, but live fully.

4 | Notoriety

One of the chief childish inclinations of our time is the love of personal publicity.

Worth

She posts then
Waits and
Watches
How many
Clicks, likes, shares
Tally to see
How well she's
Known and
Loved

This has become
The measure of her
Worth
Do more
Be more
And – by all means –
Put it on
Display

A selfie here
A clever phrase
There
Compete for the
Attention
Get the most
Views
To ensure she's
Important

What she doesn't
Realize
This isn't

Real
She's missing the
Peace
Of quiet sunsets
Roots grown in
Silence
Opting instead
For the emptiness
Of her bright
Screens

"One of the chief childish inclinations of our time is the love of personal publicity. To emerge from obscurity, to be in the public eye, to make oneself talked of — some people are so consumed with this desire that we are justified in declaring them attacked with an itch for publicity. In their eyes, obscurity is the height of disgrace. Therefore, they do their best to keep their names in every mouth.

"Politics, literature, even science, and--most odious of all--philanthropy and religion are infected by this rage for notoriety. Trumpets announce a good deed done. Pursuing its way of destruction, the rage for noise has entered places ordinarily silent, troubled spirits naturally serene, and diminished in large measure all activity for good. The abuse of showing everything, or rather, putting everything on exhibition; the growing incapacity to appreciate that which chooses to remain hidden, and the habit of estimating the value of things by the racket they make, have come to corrupt the judgment of the most earnest men, and one sometimes wonders if society will not end by transforming itself into a great fair, with each one beating his drum in front of his tent."

| 35

This is perhaps the section in Wagner's book that is the most profoundly relevant to modern times. That it was written 125 years ago is astonishing. Before Facebook, TikTok, Instagram, YouTube, Snapchat. It speaks to the fundamental nature of men and women to be seen, even revered.

So what is the central fear driving this behavior? **If I am not validated, how am I to know my worth?** One could argue that our Creator has given us intrinsic value. We are beloved. Once this truth is fully embraced, we become compelled to move beyond seeking our own worth in the approval of others and rather **act** to become all we can be.

| # Solitude

Haven

Find me here
Blond child of morning
Gray eyes searching
For gentle, soft
Mother's hands
Brushing tears away
With one smooth movement

Pick me up
Carry me out of the desert
Into cool summer sun
Wading in clean streams
Letting nature's feather fingers
Caress my curved shoulders
In the glow of daylight

Take me home
Not to the tired, rusted place
But to the new house of
Blessed brick and sturdy columns
Wrap me in safety
And sing to me of second chances
Here in my pure, hope-filled haven

"Gladly do we quit the dust and din of like exhibitions, to go and breathe peacefully in some far-off nook of the woods, all surprise that the brook is so clear, the forest so still, the solitude

so enchanting. Thank God there are yet these uninvaded corners. However formidable the uproar, however deafening the babel of clowns, it cannot carry beyond a certain limit; it grows faint and dies away. **The realm of silence is vaster than the realm of noise.** *Herein is our consolation.*

"When this intimate life loses in intensity, when man neglects it for what is superficial, he forfeits in worth all that he gains in appearance. By a sad fatality, it happens that in this way we often become less admirable in proportion as we are more admired."

The trade-off for neglecting the spiritual in favor of notoriety is often the ultimate loss of the admiration we crave. Wagner advocates finding the spiritual in solitude and nature.

Meekness

Broken

Broken
We are
Behind the
Façade
Under our
Skin

Moments of
Clarity and
Purpose
Find us
Hidden

We hang on
Tightly
Not knowing
They aren't the
Prize

Rather the
Aching
Makes us most
Alive and
Real

So let's
Surrender
To the
Strength
Masquerading as
Weakness

"In my country of Alsace, on the solitary route whose interminable ribbon stretches on and on under the forests of the Vosges, there is a stone-breaker whom I have seen at his work for thirty years. The first time I came upon him, I was a young student, setting out with swelling heart for the great city. The sight of this man did me good, for he was humming a song as he broke his stones. We exchanged a few words, and he said at the end: 'Well, good-by, my boy, good courage and good luck!' Since then I have passed and repassed along that same route, under circumstances the most diverse, painful and joyful. The student has finished his course, the breaker of stones remains what he was. He has taken a few more precautions against the seasons' storms: a rush-mat protects his back, and his felt hat is drawn further down to shield his face. But the forest is always sending back the echo of his valiant hammer. How many sudden tempests have broken over his bent back, how much adverse fate has fallen on his head, on his house, on his country! He continues to break his stones, and, coming and going I find him by the roadside, smiling in spite of his age and his wrinkles, benevolent, speaking--above all in dark days--those simple words of brave men, which have so much effect when they are scanned to the breaking of stones.

"It would be quite impossible to express the emotion the sight of this simple man gives me, and certainly he has no suspicion of it. I know of nothing more reassuring and at the same time more searching for the vanity which ferments in our hearts, than this coming face to face with an obscure worker who does his task as the oak grows and as the good God makes his sun to rise, without asking who is looking on.

"…above your gentle comings and goings, we sometimes seem to hear the rustling wings of ministering angels.

*"He who is nothing worth except on hours of parade, is worth less than nothing. Have we the perilous honor of being always in view, of marching in the front ranks? Let us take so much the greater care of the sanctuary of silent good within us. **The treasure of humanity is its hidden goodness."***

There is something holy about work done well for the simple prize of the accomplishment. How challenging it is to work in obscurity – but how rewarding the simplicity!

5 | Pride

*But that which above all
things else hinders men
from good understanding,
is pride.*

Power

"He is a
Leader"
They say
Natural-born
Commands the
Room and its
Inhabitants
Even as he
Dismisses them
They are of no
Consequence

Power is the
Jewel he
Seeks
And has
Found
But it is
Not without a
Price
His very
Soul

The illusion of
Strength he
Exhibits
Calls out for
More and
More
A beast never
Satisfied

The control he
Grasps
Like an
Addict for the
Needle
Ultimately controls
Him

"Power exercises a great influence over him who holds it. A head must be very well balanced not to be disturbed by it. The sort of dementia which took possession of the Roman emperors in the time of their world-wide rule is a universal malady whose symptoms belong to all times. In every man there sleeps a tyrant, awaiting only a favorable occasion for waking.

Power corrupts in that the control we seek eventually controls us.

"Every man who says to those dependent on him: 'Do this because it is my will and pleasure,' does ill. There is within each one of us something that invites us to resist personal power, and this something is very respectable. For at bottom we are equal, and there is no one who has the right to exact obedience from me because he is he and I am I."

"That which confers upon a man the right to demand of another the sacrifice of his time, his money, his passions, even his life, is not only that he is resolved upon all these sacrifices himself, but that he has made them in advance."

This description of a true, effective leader is one who demonstrates hard work, sacrifice, and humility. This person will never demand from others what he or she hasn't already done or is willing to do.

"To the family of the proud belong also those difficult and supersensitive people who in humble life find that their superiors never do them fitting honor, whom the best and most kindly do not succeed in satisfying, and who go about their duties with the air of a martyr."

Wagner slips in a reference to another manifestation of pride - those who complain like a martyr that they are not valued and recognized. He advocates working without attention-seeking and allowing good things to come to us even as we give of ourselves.

Walk

I walk
Feet grounded and
Eyes forward and
Steady
This route is
Clear to me
Sure of where I'm
Headed
Filled with
Purpose

I've been given
Instructions
From those with
Experience
Earned by falling
Down
Getting back up
Learning
Finding their own
Way

I grasp their reaching
Hands
Holding me and
Helping me and
Healing me
My growth is not my
Own
But more beautiful

It is all of us in
Concert

This precious and
Priceless gift of
Peace
Is not mine to
Keep
It only grows and
Fulfills and
Nurtures
When it is freely
And humbly
Given

"To resume and conclude, it is an error to think that our advantages, whatever they are, should be put to the service of our vanity. Material wealth, power, knowledge, gifts of the heart and mind, become so much cause for discord when they serve to nourish pride. They remain beneficent only so long as they are the source of modesty in those who possess them.

"Let us be humble if we have great possessions, for that proves that we are great debtors: all that a man has he owes to someone, and are we sure of being able to pay our debts?

"Let us be humble if we sit in high places and hold the fate of others in our hands; for no clear-sighted man can fail to be sensible of unfitness for so grave a role.

"Let us be humble if we have much knowledge, for it only serves to better show the vastness of the unknown, and to compare the little we have discovered for ourselves with the amplitude of that which we owe to the pains of others.

"And, above all, let us be humble if we are virtuous, since no one should be more sensible of his defects than he whose conscience is illumined, and since he more than anyone else should feel the need of charity toward evil-doers, even of suffering in their stead.

"The spirit of obedience and humility should grow with our possessions and power."

This beautiful section reminds me of the Beatitudes – profound in its simplicity. Let us be humble.

Right

I am
Right
And I stand
Strong
Secure in my
Knowledge
Trusting my
Mind

It then
Follows
You must be
Wrong
Fallacy of your
Thinking
Obvious to
Me

I lift my
Chin
Succumb to
Pride
My ego
Inflates
While empathy
Diminishes

What if I'm
Mistaken?
My line in the

Sand
Based on
Supposition
And not
Fact

Let the
Waves
Wash the line –
And my arrogance –
Away
Let me finally
Listen
With a heart that
Seeks and
Yearns for
Understanding

"But that which above all things else hinders men from good understanding, is pride.

"The last word about it is always this: If there is so much hostility and hatred between different classes of men, it is due less to exterior conditions than to an interior fatality. Conflicting interests and differences of situation dig ditches between us, it is true, but pride transforms the ditches into gulfs, and in reality it is pride alone which cries from brink to brink: 'There is nothing in common between you and us.'

Differences of opinion become weapons when pride is the driving motive behind actions.

"The sole distinction necessary is the wish to become better. The man who strives to be better becomes more humble, more approachable, more friendly even with those who owe him allegiance. But as he gains by being better known, he loses nothing in distinction, and he reaps the more respect in that he has sown the less pride."

It is in the humble striving that we grow. The unexpected byproduct of spiritual growth is the less we struggle to be known and be right, the more respected we become.

6 | Thought

*The most naive hope is nearer truth
than the most rational despair.*

| Curiosity

Focus

I am in the
Details
Digging deep
Soil overturned
To reveal
Roots
And this is
Good

But sometimes I
Wonder
Do I miss the
Point?
Looking at the
Minutia
And losing clear
Sight of the
Vision?

Lift me much
Higher
So I can see the
Truth
As an eagle spies its
Prey
Show me the
Purpose
Behind the
Work
And I will
Thrive

"Anarchy reigns in human thought: we walk in the woods, without compass or sun, lost among the brambles and briars of infinite detail.

"Thought is a tool, with its own proper function: it isn't a toy. Let us take an example. Here is the studio of a painter. The implements are all in place: everything indicates that this assemblage of means is arranged with view to an end. Throw the room open to apes. They will climb on the benches, swing from the cords, rig themselves in draperies, coif themselves with slippers, juggle with brushes, nibble the colors, and pierce the canvases to see what is behind the paint. I don't question their enjoyment; certainly they must find this kind of exercise extremely interesting. But an artist's workroom is not made to let monkeys loose in. No more is thought a ground for acrobatic evolutions. A man worthy of the name, thinks as he is, as his tastes are: he goes about it with his whole heart, and not with that fitful and sterile curiosity which, under pretext of observing and noting everything, runs the risk of never experiencing a deep and true emotion or accomplishing a right deed."

The description of apes in an artist's workroom gives an exaggerated view of what happens when we allow our curiosity to send us down rabbit holes of thought. According to a Pew Research Center survey conducted Jan. 25 to Feb. 8, 2021, 31% of U.S. adults now report that they go online "almost constantly," up from 21% in 2015. 48% say they go online several times a day. (Pew Research Center) While the study didn't focus on the content users were viewing, it is safe to assume we rarely ever leave a question unanswered because Google is **right there**. And to the mix notifications of social media posts and text interruptions, and it becomes more and more challenging to focus.

"When once man has recognized the fact that he has an aim, and that this aim is to be a man, he organizes his thought accordingly. Every mode of thinking or judging which does not make him better and stronger, he rejects as dangerous.

It is – once again – about balance. Our thoughts can serve us well and help us to become better, or they can become additional noise.

| Self-Reflection

Assessment

I take the
Assessment
Am I a
6 or 9?
INFJ?
D with secondary
S?
Perhaps an empathic
Introvert?

Who and
What am
I?
Give me the
Blueprint
Let me
Understand
What makes me
Tick

It will
Help me be
Efficient and
Effective
I'll know
What to
Say
I'll become
My absolute
Best

But this is just
Information
Helpful to a
Point
But not an
End or
Excuse or
Answer
Just one
Small part of
The greater
Story

I choose to
Set this
Self-analysis
Aside
How about
Just being
Me?
Reaching out to
Others
With no lingering
Fear

I don't need to
Understand
Why we are
The way we
Are
I just need to
Offer my
Hand
Speak imperfect
Words

From my weathered
Heart
And listen well to
Yours

"Another habit in urgent need of correction is the mania for examining and analyzing one's self at every turn. I do not invite men to neglect introspection and the examination of conscience. The endeavor to understand one's own mental attitudes and motives of conduct is an essential element of good living. But quite other is this extreme vigilance, this incessant observation of one's life and thoughts, this dissecting of one's self, like a piece of mechanism. It is a waste of time, and goes wide of the mark. The man who, to prepare himself the better for walking, should begin by making a rigid anatomical examination of his means of locomotion, would risk dislocating something before he had taken a step. You have what you need to walk with, then forward!

"It needs but a glimmer of common sense to perceive that man is not made to pass his life in a self-centered trance.

"The program of life is terribly simple, after all, and no one can put off living pending an attempt to understand life."

Self-examination is a powerful tool in helping us learn and develop. There are benefits to understanding the personalities and tendencies of others in relation to ourselves as well. The danger is in taking this introspection to an extreme and even rationalizing poor behavior by holding up a personality type as the culprit.

Again, balance is the answer. How much self-reflection serves to help us grow and serve others? The rest is just another avenue for self-absorption.

Music

Play your sweet melodies
Sing your spirit
To the open land
Beg the sky to answer
Call the thunder
Out of its hidden place

Your music is your message
The sum of your life
Praying to be heard
And answered with a teardrop
Falling from the colorless clouds
To rest on your golden arm

Tell the story of you
Woven in these lofty notes
Let them hear you
From the green mountaintops
To the flowing, satin streams
And wait for their response

When the song returns to you
On wings of raindrop fugues
Your spirit will know truth
Your voice will echo trust
And the music will take you
To the resting place that is your destiny

"But just as one need not exhaust a spring to quench his thirst, so we need not know everything to live. Humanity lives and always has lived on certain elemental **provisions**.

"First of all, humanity lives by confidence. An unshakable faith in the stability of the universe and its intelligent ordering, sleeps in everything that exists. The flowers, the trees, the beasts of the field, live in calm strength, in entire security. There is confidence in the falling rain, in dawning day, in the brook running to the sea. Everything that is seems to say: 'I am, therefore I should be; there are good reasons for this, rest assured.'"

Confidence is trust or reliance – in this case in the stability of the universe. If nature is exactly as it is meant to be, then it follows that each one of us is on this earth for a purpose.

"Deep-seated confidence is the mysterious spring that sets in motion the energy within us. It is our nutriment. By it man lives, much more than by the bread he eats. And so everything that shakes this confidence is evil--poison, not food.

"Dangerous is every system of thought that attacks the very fact of life, declaring it to be an evil.

"When one knows that certain food is dangerous to health, he does not eat it, and when a certain fashion of thinking robs us of confidence, cheerfulness and strength, we should reject that, certain not only that it is a nutriment noxious to the mind, but also that it is false. There is no truth for man but in thoughts that are human, and pessimism is inhuman."

It is possible that Wagner is writing in response to Cultural pessimism – which arises with the conviction that the culture of a nation, a civilization, or humanity itself is in a process of irreversible decline. He may also be countering the popular 19th century pessimistic views of Friedrich Nietzsche.

This pessimism can be a trap even today – pulling us down into the mire of politics and our environment, we may get so overwhelmed that we become immobile. Zooming out, we can see that history is cyclical. Yes, there are problems. But the human spirit is strong, and we are here to be a part of humanity – righting wrongs and reaching out to help others.

| Hope

Youth

You splash on
The subtle scent of youth
Gone out to play
You bathe in perfume
Of futures held
Within your fragile fingers

The world is here
Patiently tapping at
Your front door
While you sneak out the back
And tiptoe behind it
So you can own it yourself

You put the lilies
In your curls
Daisies on your wrist
And dance barefoot
Over shiny pebbles
That giggle under your feet

What a life you've given yourself
The joy of choosing
The peace of knowing
Nature's plan
You breathe in
The subtle scent of youth
That's found its home

"If mankind lives by confidence, it lives also by hope--that form of confidence which turns toward the future. All life is a result and an aspiration, all that exists supposes an origin and tends toward an end. Life is progression: progression is aspiration. The progress of the future is an infinitude of hope. Hope is at the root of things and must be reflected in the heart of man. No hope, no life. Man needs to count on tomorrow.

"Since the sun still rises, since earth puts forth her blossoms anew, since the bird builds its nest, and the mother smiles at her child, let us have the courage to be men, and commit the rest to Him who has numbered the stars. The most naive hope is nearer truth than the most rational despair."

Here is a beautiful definition of hope found in the 1939 Webster's dictionary: "The highest degree of well-founded expectation of good." Just as the sun rises, good will prevail. We just need to be willing to live in love, kindness, and trust.

7 | Speech

*Be sincere, moderate, simple in the
expression of your feelings and
opinions, in private and public alike.*

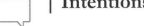

| Intentions

Whirlpool

Whirlpool
Spins and
Sucks and
Pulls me
Downward
Words in the
Water
While I
Hoped for
Truth

Will I
Let it
Own me?
Conform my
Thoughts
To the circling
Images?
How can I
Resist?

I hear the
Message
A drop among
Thousands
How do I
Know what is
Real
And not simply
Manipulation?

I will seek
Intention
Does the
Swirling
Pull me
Down or
Lift me
Up?
And what of
Those
On the same
Journey?

We will
Cleanse
In the sparkling
Streams
Search for
Goodness
Among the
Debris
Hand in
Hand
We will stay
Afloat

"Speech is the chief revelation of the mind, the first visible form that it takes. As the thought, so the speech. To better one's life in the way of simplicity, one must set a watch on his lips and his pen. Let the word be as genuine as the thought, as artless, as valid: think justly, speak frankly.

"All social relations have their roots in mutual trust, and this trust is maintained by each man's sincerity. Once sincerity diminishes, confidence is weakened, society suffers, apprehension is born. This is true in the province of both natural and spiritual interests. With people whom we distrust, it is as difficult to do business as to search for scientific truth, arrive at religious harmony, or attain to justice. When one must first question words and intentions and start from the premise that everything said and written is meant to offer us illusion in place of truth, life becomes strangely complicated. This is the case to-day. There is so much craft, so much diplomacy, so much subtle deception, that we all have no end of trouble to inform ourselves on the simplest subject and the one that most concerns us."

The tendency to "question words and intentions" has never been more widespread than today, complicating our thoughts and reducing trust to ashes.

"Formerly the means of communication between men were considerably restricted. It was natural to suppose that in perfecting and multiplying avenues of information, a better understanding would be brought about. Nations would learn to love each other as they became acquainted; citizens of one country would feel themselves bound in closer brotherhood as more light was thrown on what concerned their common life. Why should not men have reasoned thus:--'Two lights illumine better than one, and many better than two: the more periodicals and books there are, the better we shall know what happens, and those who wish to write history after us will be right fortunate; their hands will be full of documents'?

"And what has really come about is this: that quibblers, slanderers, and crooks--all gentlemen glib of tongue, who know

better than anyone else how to turn voice and pen to account—have taken the utmost advantage of these extended means for circulating thought, with the result that the men of our times have the greatest difficulty in the world to know the truth about their own age and their own affairs. For every newspaper that fosters good feeling and good understanding between nations, by trying to rightly inform its neighbors and to study them without reservations, how many spread defamation and distrust! What unnatural and dangerous currents of opinion set in motion! what false alarms and malicious interpretations of words and facts! The more newspapers one reads, the less clearly he sees in these matters.

"The result of such practices is the degradation of human speech. Men are moved only by a rage for gaining their point, or who assume that their interests are alone worth considering. Their penalty is to be forced to judge others by the rule they follow themselves: **Say what profits and not what is true.**

"What good can come from this habit of exaggerated speech? Ruffled tempers, violent and useless disputes, hasty judgments devoid of all moderation--these things are the result of intemperance of speech.

"To him who has preserved enough honesty, nothing is more repugnant than the careless irony of an acrobat of the tongue or pen, who tries to dupe honest and ingenuous men."

This is another section surprising in its relevance to the situation we experience today amid the vast information at our fingertips. "*The more newspapers one reads, the less clearly he sees in these matters.*" This truth is profound. Should we believe CNN or Fox News? Shall we go down the conspiracy theory rabbit hole? Google any topic, and you will find seemingly indisputable proof in support of any viewpoint. The "*degradation of human speech*" inevitably results. A heavy curtain of fog descends, and words become meaningless.

"This is the crime of those who distort and degrade speech: they shake confidence generally. We consider as a calamity the debasement of the currency, the lowering of interest, the abolition of credit:--there is a misfortune greater than these: the loss of confidence, of that moral credit which honest people give one another, and which makes speech circulate like an authentic currency. Away with the makers of counterfeit speech, for because of them there is no longer confidence in anyone or anything, and what they say and write is worthless."

The result of all this noise – the loss of confidence. Wagner has already established that confidence is an elemental provision for living (Chapter 6 - Thought). Shaking this calm strength is dangerous indeed. It breeds fear, and we are left clamoring for something to hold onto and distancing from each other in the process.

| Sincerity

Words

Your words are
Powerful
They can fill a
Cup
Or cut to
Ribbons
They are pristine
Truth
Or manipulative
Lies
Examine the
Heart
Before words are
Formed
Consider the
Impact
And choose
Wisely

"You see how urgent it is that each should guard his lips, chasten his pen, and aspire to simplicity of speech. No more perversion of sense, indirectness, reticence, evasion! These things serve only to complicate and bewilder. Be men; speak the speech of honor. An hour of plain dealing does more for the salvation of the world than years of duplicity.

"The greatest things are those which gain the most by being said most simply, since thus they show themselves for what they are.

Nothing so strong, nothing so persuasive, as simplicity! To be convincing, a thing must be true, and certain truths are more evident when they come in the speech of innocence, even weakness, than when they fall from lips too well trained, or are proclaimed with trumpets. Be sincere, moderate, simple in the expression of your feelings and opinions, in private and public alike."

Wagner set the stage with an indictment of ill-intentioned voices in the last section. Here he provides the remedy. Exercise a measure of self-control at times, be direct and sincere in communication, and aspire to simplicity of speech.

| Goodness

Loved

It was there
A warm, welcoming voice
Both in her and around her
The words – "You are loved"
Never had she felt it
Never had she known it
Truly, deeply
In her whole self –
Not just her mind

Finally, no resisting
Just tears
Washing away the wrongs
Cleansing, healing, moving
Her to newness
"You are loved"
In spite of all
In place of all
Just as she was
And all she would become

The words gave her freedom
Unlocked the doors
Flung them open
And sent her – laughing –
Out into this bright world
Never to be alone again

"Another source of light on the path of human life is goodness. Given the unknown brooding above our heads, our limited intelligence, the grievous and contradictory enigma of human destiny, falsehood, hatred, corruption, suffering, death--what can we think, what do? To all these questions a sublime and mysterious voice has answered: **Love your fellow-men.** *Love must indeed be divine, like faith and hope, since she cannot die when so many powers are arrayed against her. She has to combat the natural ferocity of what may be called the beast in man; she has to meet ruse, force, self-interest, above all, ingratitude.*

"At the very heart of the Christian faith, the most sublime of its teachings, and to him who penetrates its deepest sense, the most human, is this: To save lost humanity, the invisible God came to dwell among us, in the form of a man, and willed to make Himself known by this single sign: **Love.**

"Healing, consoling, tender to the unfortunate, even to the evil, love engenders light beneath her feet. She clarifies, she simplifies. She has chosen the humblest part--to bind up wounds, wipe away tears, relieve distress, soothe aching hearts, pardon, make peace; yet it is of love that we have the greatest need. And as we meditate on the best way to render thought fruitful, simple, really conformable to our destiny, the method sums itself up in these words: **Have confidence and hope; be kind.**"

Gratitude breeds goodness. The more grateful we are for our lives, family, and friends, the more love we have to give. A psychological study in 2006 (Bartlett and DeSteno) found that beneficiaries of a kind act who were grateful were more inclined to help a stranger who had not helped them compared to individuals who were not grateful.

God

Is this your
God?
One of
Cruelty and
Differences?
This deity sows
Dissent
I want no
Part

I found my
God
In the crippled
Hands
Of the
Beggar
Willing to
Share his
Morsels

I found my
God
In the open
Heart
Of the
Woman
Protecting me
With her
Mask

I found my
God
In the opposing
Voice
Of the
Man
Sharing his
Views with
Kindness

This is the
God
I will hold
Onto
Through the
Growing pains
Of a hurting
People
This is the
Goodness I
Seek and
This is the
God I
Trust

"Since I have touched here upon religious ground, at least in a general way, someone may ask me to say in a few simple words, what religion is the best. It is better to put the question otherwise, and ask: Is my own religion good, and how may I know it? To this question, this answer: Your religion is good if it is vital and active, if it nourishes in you confidence, hope, love, and a sentiment of the infinite value of existence; if it is allied with what is best in you against what is worst, and holds forever

before you the necessity of becoming a new man; if it makes you understand that pain is a deliverer; if it increases your respect for the conscience of others; if it renders forgiveness more easy, fortune less arrogant, duty more dear, the beyond less visionary. If it does these things it is good, little matter its name: however rudimentary it may be, when it fills this office it comes from the true source, it binds you to man and to God."

This beautiful description of religion at its best is rich with truth. Consider the phrase: "If it makes you understand that pain is a deliverer." We spend a great deal of time and effort avoiding and/or trying to lesson pain. But the greatest spiritual growth can result from the greatest pain. And Wagner digs even deeper by using the word deliverer. Deliver – to free; to release, as from restraint; to set at liberty; to rescue or save. Experiencing hurt and allowing God and others into that space frees us from self-reliance. Sharing personal pain connects us in a deep, vulnerable way. We need community and to know that we are never alone.

"But does it perchance serve to make you think yourself better than others, quibble over texts, wear sour looks, domineer over others' consciences or give your own over to bondage; stifle your scruples, follow religious forms for fashion or gain, do good in the hope of escaping future punishment?--oh, then, if you proclaim yourself the follower of Buddha, Moses, Mahomet, or even Christ, your religion is worthless--it separates you from God and man."

There is so much division in the name of religion today. This arrogance results in separation from each other when what we need to thrive is true human as well as spiritual connectedness.

| 79

8 | Family

But whence does the individual draw his originality--this unique something, which, joined to the distinctive qualities of others, constitutes the wealth and strength of a community? He can draw it only from his own family.

Orleans

Bulb flashes
Captures this moment
These three
Sitting, laughing
Telling stories
Of war fought on muddy land
Of music from the soul
Of younger years and love

He talks for hours
Grayed head and gnarled hands
But voice as clear as a boy's
He shares his wisdom
And stubborn foolishness of youth
While I sit, wide-eyed,
Wondering how I lucked into this place
Willing my mind to remember every detail
Cherishing every syllable

She is still vivacious
Enjoying the band
As it recalls the tunes of 40 years passed
Her face reveals few wrinkles
For all she's seen
And her heart bounces
Across the room this night

We each tell who we are
Amid the pink steak and buttery fish
Served to us by skilled hands

The sweet chocolate dessert
Is surpassed by the sweetness
Of this time
Our time – together

This is too perfect to have been planned
We walk out of the oak doors
Into the night
And take with us the joy
Of sharing from the heart
Of learning to listen
Of celebrating in love
As a family

"Family feeling, like all beautiful things, has its caricature, which is family egoism. Some families are like barred and bolted citadels, their members organized for the exploitation of the whole world. Everything that does not directly concern them is indifferent to them.

Just as with anything else, being laser-focused on self (whether individual, family, or nation) can lead to isolation and pride.

"But whence does the individual draw his originality--this unique something, which, joined to the distinctive qualities of others, constitutes the wealth and strength of a community? He can draw it only from his own family.

"And the very base of family feeling is respect for the past; for the best possessions of a family are its common memories. An intangible, indivisible and inalienable capital, these souvenirs constitute a sacred fund that each member of a family ought to

consider more precious than anything else he possesses. They
exist in a dual form: in idea and in fact. They show themselves
in language, habits of thought, sentiments, even instincts, and
one sees them materialized in portraits, furniture, buildings,
dress, songs. To profane eyes, they are nothing; to the eyes of
those who know how to appreciate the things of the family, they
are relics with which one should not part at any price."

We all have treasures – a grandfather's watch, a mother's
ring, hand-written letters yellowed with age. They might
be tucked away in a hand-carved box, brought out from
time to time to stir memories and hearts. Families –
whether families of origin or those made up of friends
chosen in adulthood – have a uniqueness about them.
They speak a language of their own that is priceless to the
members. Wagner asserts that the joining of each
distinctive family is what constitutes a society and that its
strength lies in the differences brought together to make
up the whole.

Cracks

My fingers
Trace the
Cracks
Feel the
Ceramic
Splits
Where once
This bowl was
Solid

These grooves
Tell the
Story of
Use and
Purpose and
Meaning
Found in this
Vessel

Should it
Now simply be
Discarded?
Substance once
Held
Now seeping
Through its
Crevices?

Like us
It is
Worn

But perhaps
Made more
Beautiful
In the
Wearing

Lines suggesting
Life
Beauty in the
Brokenness
And held
Together by
Shared and
Treasured
Memories

"To create a home you must have the spirit of home. Just as the smallest village may have its history, its moral stamp, so the smallest home may have its soul. "It is said that walls have ears. They have also voices, a mute eloquence. Everything that a dwelling contains is bathed in an ether of personality.

"Words can do little justice to the subject of home, tell little about the effect of a favorite flower in the window, or the charm of an old arm-chair where the grandfather used to sit, offering his wrinkled hands to the kisses of chubby children.

"Poor moderns, always moving or remodeling!

"The worldly spirit is full of impertinences. It finds everything out of date, awkward, too simple, lacking the modern touch.

"Many young people when they marry, listen to this voice of the world. Their parents have given them the example of a modest life; but the new generation thinks it affirms its rights to existence and liberty, by repudiating ways in its eyes too patriarchal. So these young folks make efforts to set themselves up lavishly in the latest fashion, and rid themselves of useless property at dirt-cheap prices. Instead of filling their houses with objects which say: Remember! they garnish them with quite new furnishings that as yet have no meaning."

Certainly, letting go of old, damaged items is healthy. However, Wagner makes a point here. Are we always looking for something better, sacrificing the beautiful that we already possess? Are we so obsessed with remodels, transformations, old made new that we forget there is a certain sanctity in reverence for worn, lived-in spaces? Can we appreciate the chipped bowl filled with salad, the softened leather of a couch as we sink into it? If we are made more beautiful by our brokenness, is there not value to be found in solid pieces weathered by family stories and memories?

"The home, then, becomes a sort of half-way house where one comes to rest a little between two prolonged absences; it isn't a good place to stay. As it has no soul, it does not speak to yours. Time to eat and sleep, and then off again!

"We are all acquainted with people who have a rage for being abroad, who think the world would no longer go round if they didn't figure on all sides of it. To stay at home is penal; there they cease to be in view. A horror of home life possesses them to such a degree that they would rather pay to be bored outside than be amused gratuitously within."

"We too much resemble those people who claim the rights of family only to gain advantage from them, not to do honor to the connection.

A lesson from Covid is that our homes can be a haven of comfort if we are able slow down enough to appreciate them.

Hands

Hands
Soft and young and agile
Mix white plaster
Spread and smooth and sand
Walls once cracked
Restored to newness
Coat on coat of pale paint
Covers empty surfaces
Brushed by joyous siblings'
Hands

Hands
Strong and nurturing and vibrant
Fall into a cadence
Melt chocolate over low heat
Stir and beat and whip
Until the gloss is gone
And thick fudge remains
Liquid slowly poured into pan
Squares cut by meticulous Mother's
Hands

Hands
Crippled and caring and worn
Lift the innocent toddler
Into his comforting lap
Sing and laugh and tickle
Play harmonica and tell jokes
Give the child boundless love
And steady certainty

Safely held in gracious Father's
Hands

Hands
Graceful and melodic and nimble
Skim over ivory keys
Coax and craft and create
Moving music and
Sacred beauty in sound
Notes bounce off wooden beams
And fill the halls and stairwell
As songs are formed by gifted brother's
Hands

Hands
Sensitive and tender and kind
Wipe the falling tear
From my despairing eyes
Defend and comfort and understand
The aching of a broken heart
Sit silently in precious stillness
Reach and intertwine
My fingers with a cherished sister's
Hands

Hands
Old and young and growing
Work in concert
Peel the green outer layer
Exposing hardened shell
Crack and pick and sample
The pecan's sweet meat
This circle keeps a place
For every family member
These words preserve our memory

Of simple days together
And this love holds our hearts
In timeless and treasured
Hands

"In general, but two methods of rearing children are practiced: the first is to bring them up for ourselves; the second, to bring them up for themselves.

"In the first case the child is looked upon as a complement of the parents: he is part of their property, occupies a place among their possessions. As he grows older, this subordination becomes a veritable confiscation, extending to his ideas, his feelings, everything. Instead of slowly evolving into independence, the man advances into slavery. He is what he is permitted to be, what his father's business, religious beliefs, political opinions or esthetic tastes require him to be. He will think, speak, act, and marry according to the understanding and limits of the paternal absolutism. That he should live in them, through them, for them, is the only thing admissible.

"The other system is the extreme opposite, that of bringing up children for themselves. The roles are reversed: the parents are there for the child. No sooner is he born than he becomes the center. The newcomer is not long in discovering his omnipotence, and before he can walk he is drunken with it. As he grows older all this deepens and broadens. Parents, grandparents, servants, teachers, everybody is at his command. There is only himself. He is the unique, the perfect, the infallible. Too late it is perceived that all this has been evolving a master; and what a master! forgetful of sacrifices, without respect, even pity. He no longer has any regard for those to

whom he owes everything, and he goes through life without law or check."

Wagner presents two opposing styles of parenting – both, in his view, missing the mark. In the first, the child is viewed as an extension of the parents; in the second, the center of the family. Both are extremes, so where do we find balance in bringing up our children?

"Children should be educated neither for themselves nor for their parents: They should be educated for life. At no moment of their direction over him can parents forget that this little being confided to their care must become himself and a brother.

"He who is free and strong is unflinching in speech. We should encourage in our children the hardihood to speak frankly.

"To watch, to guide, to keep a firm hand--such is the function of the educator."

The balance is found in recognizing that children should learn to live as a member of society. We must do our best to instill a sense of duty, responsibility, and kindness towards others. We can also encourage our children to speak their truth, even as they are working it out and learning who they are and their place in society.

"To watch, to guide, to keep a firm hand…" I have an old, tiny New Testament that my father took to World War II with him. In it is a handwritten quote: "A good parent: one who makes himself or herself progressively unnecessary." When we are at our best as parents, we allow our children more and more freedom to make their own decisions while we're still there to catch them when they fall, thus equipping them to live without us.

9 | Mission

Work out your mission.

Fractured

Fractured
One nation
Divisible
Hatred and
Anger and
Strife
I am tired of
Being hostile
But kindness
Brought no
Change

Is it more
Caring to
Challenge?
Or do I
Surrender to
Inequity?
Love is not
Silence
I must find
Courage

But the
Gauntlet is
First
Thrown to me
Self-examination
Leaves me
Raw
I have been

Part of the
Problem

Lay my soul
Bare
Tell the
Stories of my
Youth
Ugly tales of
When color
Mattered to
Me
I am
Ashamed

There are those
Who are
Abandoned
I will join
My new-found
Voice with
Theirs
So the sound
Will shake the
Earth and
Cause an
Avalanche

We are
Fractured
But my
Hope is
Steadfast
If I must
Struggle

I will
With one goal
In mind
Justice for
All

"Need we say that one does not rise to this point of view without a struggle? The spirit of simplicity is not an inherited gift, but the result of a laborious conquest. Plain living, like high thinking, is simplification. The moral life begins in a certain confusion, makes trial of itself, seeks to understand itself, and often mistakes. But by force of action, and exacting from himself strict account of his deeds, man arrives at a better knowledge of life. Its law appears to him, and the law is this:- **Work out your mission.** *He who applies himself to aught else than the realization of this end, loses in living the raison d'être of life. The egoist does so, the pleasure-seeker, the ambitious: he consumes existence as one eating the full corn in the blade,--he prevents it from bearing its fruit; his life is lost.*

This is the crux of it. Apply ourselves to finding and fulfilling our purpose. But how do we work out our mission? Wagner advocates connecting to nature and to God. Being in silence away from distractions allows a quieting of the mind to hear one's inner voice. The unfolding of purpose is a lifelong pursuit. But a start – however small – is necessary before we begin to simplify with any clear direction.

"Whoever makes his life serve a good higher than itself, saves it in giving it. Moral precepts, which to a superficial view appear arbitrary, and seem made to spoil our zest for life, have really

| 98

but one object--to preserve us from the evil of having lived in vain. That is why they are constantly leading us back into the same paths; that is why they all have the same meaning: **Do not waste your life,** *make it bear fruit; learn how to give it, in order that it may not consume itself! Herein is summed up the experience of humanity, and this experience, which each man must remake for himself, is more precious in proportion as it costs more dear. Illumined by its light, he makes a moral advance more and more sure. Now he has his means of orientation, his internal norm to which he may lead everything back; and from the vacillating, confused, and complex being that he was, he becomes simple. By the ceaseless influence of this same law, which expands within him, and is day by day verified in fact, his opinions and habits become transformed."*

Wagner points out that this inner light orients and guides one's actions. Once we even have an inkling of our life's purpose, superfluous activities become less enticing. As he puts it –habits become transformed. We can read hundreds of self-help books, make lists, and create vision boards, but without clarity of purpose, we won't be **internally transformed**.

And this important sentence is grounding. "Do not waste your life, make it bear fruit; learn how to give it, in order that it may not consume itself!" It truly is in giving that we are fulfilled.

"Once captivated by the beauty and sublimity of the true life, by what is sacred and pathetic in this strife of humanity for truth, justice, and brotherly love, his heart holds the fascination of it. Gradually everything subordinates itself to this powerful and persistent charm. The necessary hierarchy of powers is organized

| 99

within him: the essential commands, the secondary obeys, and order is born of simplicity. We may compare this organization of the interior life to that of an army. An army is strong by its discipline, and its discipline consists in respect of the inferior for the superior, and the concentration of all its energies toward a single end: discipline once relaxed, the army suffers. It will not do to let the corporal command the general. Examine carefully your life and the lives of others. Whenever something halts or jars, and complications and disorder follow, it is because the corporal has issued orders to the general. Where the natural law rules in the heart, disorder vanishes."

Here he provides a barometer to show when we're getting off track. When scattered and undisciplined, we've most likely allowed the secondary to take precedence over the essential. This is going to happen often – it's just human nature. There is no reason to beat ourselves up over it. We just begin anew. That's the beauty of life – just as the sun rises each day, we can start over anytime we find ourselves wandering from our purpose.

Stone

I carry the
Boulder
Red clay
Solid
And deposit it
Gently
In its resting
Place

More rocks will
Follow
Various hues and
Shapes
But they will
Land
In a spot of my
Choosing

My back is
Weary
Strong arms
Aching
But I will
Persevere
Because I have a
Vision

My work is
Destiny
My heart
Pure
I live this
Mission

In these contours of
Stone

"The best we put into our work--be that work done by strength of muscle, warmth of heart, or concentration of mind--is precisely that for which no one can pay us. Nothing better proves that man is not a machine than this fact: two men at work with the same forces and the same movements, produce totally different results. Where lies the cause of this phenomenon? In the divergence of their intentions. One has the mercenary spirit, the other has singleness of purpose. Both receive their pay, but the labor of the one is barren; the other has put his soul into his work. The work of the first is like a grain of sand, out of which nothing comes through all eternity; the other's work is like the living seed thrown into the ground; it germinates and brings forth harvests. This is the secret which explains why so many people have failed while employing the very processes by which others succeed. Automatons do not reproduce their kind, and mercenary labor yields no fruit.

"Those who make the least noise do the most work."

No matter what the job is at the moment, giving our best (which can be different on any given day) yields a measure of gratification. Brother Lawrence, the 17th century monk who found spirituality in the ordinary task of washing dishes in his monastery, said that our sanctification did not depend as much on changing our activities as it does on doing them for God rather than for ourselves. Whether in the perfect job at the moment or not, one can find value and motivation in the work.

"Fidelity in small things is at the base of every great achievement. We too often forget this, and yet no truth needs more to be kept in mind, particularly in the troubled eras of history and in the crises of individual life. In shipwreck a splintered beam, an oar, any scrap of wreckage, saves us. On the tumbling waves of life, when everything seems shattered to fragments, let us not forget that a single one of these poor bits may become our plank of safety. To despise the remnants is demoralization.

"In general, those who lose their souls do so not because they fail to rise to difficult duty, but because they neglect to perform that which is simple."

Here Wagner warns us not to neglect to take care of the little things. This cultivates discipline. And we can never know when small actions will have a great impact.

Enough

There may be a time when
Peaceful waters run
From nation to nation
And children's tears are wiped
With a tender, loving hand
And there is plenty to go around

There may be
Wonders we never imagined
Awaiting us over the next hill
And holding us in their sights
And we may all be happy someday

Maybe now we have to settle for
A baby's soft cooing
And orange leaves in the fall
And doors held open by strangers' hands
And maybe – for this one brief moment –
That will have to be enough

"One never pays too dear for the conviction that there are things which money will not buy."

We must pursue who and what we are created to be with more fervor than we pursue material prosperity. But it's difficult to experience this with any consistency absent a core heart change.

"The most beautiful acts of service and the hardest tasks have generally little remuneration or none.

"Be at once rich and simple...consider your wealth as a means of fulfilling your mission in the world."

Wagner gives us a clear action to take in pursuit of this goal. The core heart change comes in the form of clarity of purpose. Once I know my mission in the world, it becomes my true north. From that point on, the decision to obtain material goods becomes a simple one: does this support my mission or not?

10 | Simplicity

Simplicity is a state of mind.

⚓ | **Virtues**

Comfort

Dust on ivory keys
Whispers of a melody
Somehow locked

Slick white pages
Phrases unwritten
Somewhere hidden

And I sit on the floor
Hoping for the courage
To open myself

I know the flood of feeling
Born from a single note
Hammer hitting strings

I know the gentle release
Arising from a single word
Ink flowing on paper

It's enough for me
To play a melody
No one can hear
In my darkened room

It's enough for me
To reach for a pen
And let the words flow
When the pain is too much

I'll stroke those keys
And let my music free
I'll capture stirring images
And set my soul free
And in this simple creation
I'll find my comfort

⚓

"Simplicity is a state of mind. It dwells in the main intention of our lives."

Once our mission comes into focus and anything that doesn't fall in line with that mission falls away, we are left with simplicity.

"A man is simple when his chief care is the wish to be what he ought to be, that is, honestly and naturally human. At bottom, it consists in putting our acts and aspirations in accordance with the law of our being, and consequently with the Eternal Intention which willed that we should be at all.

"The human ideal is to transform life into something more excellent than itself. We may compare existence to raw material. What it is matters less than what is made of it, as the value of a work of art lies in the flowering of the workman's skill. We bring into the world with us different gifts: one has received gold, another granite, a third marble, most of us wood or clay. Our task is to fashion these substances. Everyone knows that the most precious material may be spoiled, and he knows, too, that out of the least costly an immortal work may be shaped. **Art is the realization of a permanent idea in an ephemeral form.** *True life is the realization of the*

higher virtues,--justice, love, truth, liberty, moral power,--in our daily activities, whatever they may be. And this life is possible in social conditions the most diverse, and with natural gifts the most unequal. It is not fortune or personal advantage, but our turning them to account, that constitutes the value of life. Fame adds no more than does length of days: quality is the thing."

Wagner compares living out an ideal to art. Just as an artist brings a vision to fruition in artwork, we bring our best selves and truest ideas and fashion a life. "True life is the realization of the higher virtues – justice, love, truth, liberty, moral power – in our daily activities, whatever they may be." The motivation behind the action of doing what is in front of us in the moment is key to the end result.

Roots

Solid ground
Smooth stone
And I stand
Sure-footed
Supported by
Who I am
And I know
Her
Now

But what if
Uncertainty Comes
Different and
Challenging and
Strong
What if I
Weaken

Hard rock
Melting into
Quicksand
Swallowing the
Me
I thought I
Knew

Will even this
Face
Be revealed
As a
Façade

Covering the
Hole
Where my
Soul should
Be?

Help me
Trust
That I will not
Shrink
That if my
Foundation
Crumbles and
Leaves me
On the
Ground

I will
Rise and
Learn and
Seek until
I find inner
Peace
And in this
Transformation
I will grow
Roots

⚓

"Whether it be a question of food, dress, or dwelling, simplicity of taste is also a source of independence and safety. The more simply you live, the more secure is your future; you are less at the mercy of surprises and reverses. An illness or a period of idleness does not suffice to dispossess you: a change of position,

even considerable, does not put you to confusion. Having simple needs, you find it less painful to accustom yourself to the hazards of fortune. You remain a man, though you lose your office or your income, because the foundation on which your life rests is not your table, your cellar, your horses, your goods and chattels, or your money. In adversity you will not act like a nursling deprived of its bottle and rattle."

Wagner iterates the benefits of simple living in that (assuming basic needs are met) living below our means provides a sort of liberty. When hard times invariably come, we're able to weather the storms without losing our footing.

"Liberty is an atmosphere of the higher life, and it is only by a slow and patient inward transformation that one becomes capable of breathing it. The man who guides his life by inner law, can no more live servile to outward authority than can the full-grown bird live imprisoned in the eggshell. But the man who has not yet attained to governing himself can no more live under the law of liberty than can the unfledged bird live without its protective covering."

Here he takes liberty beyond the material – that in finding inward peace through simplicity, we attain a type of freedom. Yet another divine twist – in focusing on a mission and giving up distractions, we are freed to pursue the abundance around us like a bird being freed from its shell.

Portal

I found your
Music
In my soul
It planted and
Grew there
Full and
Flowering and
Painful
And sent me
Searching

I want to
Know
This world of
Struggle and
Striving and
Strength
Driven by
Respect
So I won't be
Separate

Art is my
Portal
Melodies and
Words and
Paintings
That take me
Deeper into this
Realm

Further into
Beauty

History breathes
Life
Into each
Moment
Informs my
Future
And leads me to
Understanding
I am forever
Changed

"The spirit of simplicity is not an inherited gift, but the result of a laborious conquest.

"If nothing but a branch is left for you to cling to, cling to that branch; and if you stand alone in defense of a losing cause, do not throw down your arms to join the rout. The future sometimes rests in a single life as truly as life sometimes hangs by a thread. For strength, go to history and Nature. From the long travail of both you will learn that failure and fortune alike may come from the slightest cause, that it is not wise to neglect detail, and, above all, that we must know how to wait and to begin again."

We are reminded to stand strong in defense of noble causes. And if failure comes, we can begin again. All that is required is willingness, and we become stronger through the effort.

Sunlight

There is a
Darkness
It hovers and
Covers and
Cloaks
Keeps beauty
Suppressed
And pushes her
Down

If only she
Knew
The hidden and
Deepening
Hues
That come from
Within
And beg to be
Seen

Sunlight over the
Mountain
Creeps and
Comes and
Illuminates
She is
Shown and
Known and
Beautiful

There is a
Richness
Dark places

Lighted and
Revealed are
Cherished
For her colorful
Strength now
Visible

"I despair of ever describing simplicity in any worthy fashion. All the strength of the world and all its beauty, all true joy, everything that consoles, that feeds hope, or throws a ray of light along our dark paths, everything that makes us see across our poor lives a splendid goal and a boundless future, comes to us from people of simplicity, those who have made another object of their desires than the passing satisfaction of selfishness and vanity, and have understood that the art of living is to know how to give one's life.

That beautiful paradox presents itself: **I am fulfilled when I give.** As we begin to work towards our purpose, self-absorption naturally falls away. We move closer and closer to what we were made to be – individually and collectively.

⚓ | Marvel

Maypole

Maypole
Stands tall
In the
Welcoming
Warmth of the
Sun
Ribbons extend
To our outstretched
Hands
And we
Begin to
Move

Our bare
Feet
Flutter lightly
Over soft
Earth
The music is
Alive
Within us
And we are
Free

This dance
Is our
Prayer
Lifts and
Sways and
Moves us
As our

Arms and
Hearts
Almost touch the
Sky

Our faces are
Flushed
From the
Laughter and
Summer
Heat
Our bodies
Joined to the
Source
And to each
Other

As the
Sun sets
We slow and
Rest
Our spirits
Smile
At the
Communion
Of our
True
Selves

Our souls now
Nourished
We leave this
Place
Not empty-
Handed

But with the
Cherished
Memory
Of this glorious
Day we
Danced

"Wherever life is simple and sane, true pleasure accompanies it as fragrance does uncultivated flowers.

"It is time to become little children once more, to learn again to stand with clasped hands and wide eyes before the mystery around us; to remember that, in spite of our knowledge, what we know is but a trifle, and that the world is greater than our mind.

"I ask indulgence for everything naïve and simple, not alone for the innocent conceits that flutter round the curly heads of children, but also for the legend, the folk song, the tales of the world of marvel and mystery. The sense of the marvelous is in the child the first form of that sense of the infinite without which a man is like a bird deprived of wings.

"Nature gives us her example, and the man who should affect contempt for the ephemeral splendor of beauty with which we garnish our brief days, would lose sight of the intentions of Him who has put the same care and love into the painting of the lily of an hour and the eternal hills."

Throughout Wagner's life, he espoused a simple faith without dogma and a love of nature. He notes in his book

"The Voice of Nature", "All creation speaks to him who knows how to lend his ear."

"The beauty and poetry of existence lie in the understanding we have of it.

"Poetry is not in things; it is in us. It must be impressed on objects from without, as the sculptor impresses his dream on the marble. If our life and our occupations remain too often without charm, in spite of any outward distinction they may have, it is because we have not known how to put anything into them.

To be one's self, to realize in one's natural place the kind of beauty which is fitting there--this is the ideal. "

This simple life – driven by purpose and inspired by wonder – is an ideal worth the striving.

11 | Society

The spirit of simplicity is a great magician. It softens asperities, bridges chasms, draws together hands and hearts. This is the true social cement, that goes into the building of a people.

 **| Others**

Sit

Sit with me
Hold my hand
Let me cry
And do not
Wipe away my tears

Let the soothing
Be in the sharing
Heart to heart
Pain met fully
And felt fully

This is relationship
Not an erasing
Of the soul-searing hurt
But a walking through
Together

"We are not simple enough to be happy and to render others so. We lack the singleness of heart and the self-forgetfulness. We spread joy, as we do consolation, by such methods as to obtain negative results. To console a person, what do we do? We set to work to dispute his suffering, persuade him that he is mistaken in thinking himself unhappy. In reality, our language translated into truthful speech would amount to this: 'You suffer, my friend? That is strange; you must be mistaken, for I feel nothing.' As the only human means of soothing grief is to share

*it in the heart, how must a sufferer feel, consoled in this
fashion?*

*"And when people whom you know are in trial, do not draw a
sanitary cordon round them--as though they had the plague--
that you cross only with precautions which recall to them their
sad lot. On the contrary, after showing all your sympathy, all
your respect for their grief, comfort them, help them to take up
life again; carry them a breath from the out-of-doors--something
in short to remind them that their misfortune does not shut
them off from the world."*

This is such a good reminder. We are not called to erase
the pain of others but rather acknowledge it, sit with them
through it, and then help them ease back into life.

*"To give pleasure to others and take it ourselves, we have to
begin by removing the ego, which is hateful, and then keep it in
chains as long as the diversions last. There is no worse killjoy
than the ego. We must be good children, sweet and kind, button
our coats over our medals and titles, and with our whole heart
put ourselves at the disposal of others.*

*"How much better would one understand another if he knew
how to put himself heartily in that other's place, and how much
more pleasure there would be in life!*

*"No one seems to doubt the immense human interest attached
to joy. It is a sacred flame that must be fed, and that throws a
splendid radiance over life. He who takes pains to foster it
accomplishes a work as profitable for humanity as he who
builds bridges, pierces tunnels, or cultivates the ground. So to
order one's life as to keep, amid toils and suffering, the faculty*

of happiness, and be able to propagate it in a sort of salutary contagion among one's fellow-men, is to do a work of fraternity in the noblest sense. To give a trifling pleasure, smooth an anxious brow, bring a little light into dark paths--what a truly divine office in the midst of this poor humanity! But it is only in great simplicity of heart that one succeeds in filling it.

"Let us sometimes live--be it only for an hour, and though we must lay all else aside--to make others smile."

The essence of community is described here. Let go of self-centeredness and help others. Walk together through joys and sorrows. Cultivate – and share – the faculty of happiness.

◈ | Nation

911

It hit her
That moment of knowing
Lives were being lost
Last breaths
Letting go

Their fight was over
Buried in the rubble
No rescue
Some would remain
And she cried for them

Strangers
Yet brothers, sisters
Lost in a war
Unknown to all of us
Until that day

She had to sing
To pray the word
To carry their souls
From this world
To a place of peace

And in those minutes
She was with them
Holding them in
Her heart
And the tears fell again

"In a lecture delivered in 1882, M. Renan said that a nation is 'a spiritual family,' and he added: 'The essential of a nation is that all the individuals should have many things in common, and also that all should have forgotten much.' It is important to know what to forget and what to remember, not only in the past, but also in our daily life. **Our memories are lumbered with the things that divide us; the things which unite us slip away.**

"So too do we foster bad feeling in our brothers. Men animated by a spirit of particularism, exclusiveness, and pride, are continually clashing. They cannot meet without rousing afresh the sentiment of division and rivalry. And so there slowly heaps up in their remembrance a stock of reciprocal ill-will, of mistrust, of rancor. All this is bad feeling with its consequences.

"It must be rooted out of our midst. Remember, forget! This we should say to ourselves every morning, in all our relations and affairs. Remember the essential, forget the accessory! How much better should we discharge our duties as citizens, if high and low were nourished from this spirit! How easy to cultivate pleasant remembrances in the mind of one's neighbor, by sowing it with kind deeds and refraining from procedures of which in spite of himself he is forced to say, with hatred in his heart: 'Never in the world will I forget!'"

This one is a challenge. There are things worth the fight: ending racism, taking care of the oppressed, saving our children from senseless gun violence, to name a few. But alienating those that would join in the fight is counterproductive.

"If the spirit of caste causes the loss of respect, partisanship - of whatever sort - is quite as productive of it. In certain quarters children are brought up in such fashion that they respect but one country--their own; one system of government--that of their parents and masters; one religion--that which they have been taught. Does anyone suppose that in this way men can be shaped who shall respect country, religion, and law? **Is this a proper respect--this respect which does not extend beyond what touches and belongs to ourselves?** *Strange blindness of cliques, which demand for themselves respect and which, outside themselves, respect nothing. In reality they teach: 'Country, religion, law--we are all these!' Such teaching fosters fanaticism, and if fanaticism is not the sole anti-social cause, it is surely one of the worst and most energetic."*

Wagner ties national egoism to fanaticism. Let's take the leap with him. If we believe that everything our political party or country does is right and that our religion is the one and only way to God, we are blinded and blocked from learning anything new. Digging our heels in further, we are in danger of becoming extremists.

Responsibility

Moment

At this very moment
There is a family
Standing in a hospital waiting room
Too nervous to sit
Too scared to leave
Unsure of every step
As they pace
And wait
To hear whether she will live or die

At this very moment
There is a couple
Whose naked bodies are entwined
In rapturous lovemaking
Their minds and bodies
Are absorbed with each other
And the kisses
And the touches
Belong to the joining of their existence

At this very moment
There is a man
Sitting on a street corner
Sign held by his beggar's hands
His mind cannot hold a thought
And fear has become his soulmate
And he waits
And hopes
For enough coins to sustain him through the night

At this very moment
There is a baby
Fighting her way through her mother's womb
Moving to find what awaits outside
And her mind cannot know
And her heart cannot sense
The comfort
And love
That will beckon from her mother's eyes

At this very moment
There is a man
Whose body is weakened
Who suffers constant pain
And he is ready to reach the end
Or beginning
And he prays
And he looks
To find the passage to another life

At this very moment
There is excruciating pain
And unspeakable joy
Cruelty and compassion
There is love with no boundaries
And hatred that rolls in like fog
And we are all a part of it
And it is in our bones
And this sharing of humanity –
This is life

*"I knew a man to whom every misfortune had come which can
strike us in our affections. He had lost a beloved wife, had seen*

all his children buried, one after another. But he had a great fortune, the result of his own labor. Living in the utmost simplicity, almost without personal wants, he spent his time in searching for opportunities to do good and profiting by them. How many people he surprised in flagrant poverty, what means he combined for relieving distress and lighting up dark lives, with what kindly thoughtfulness he took his friends unawares, no one can imagine. He liked to do good to others and enjoy their surprise when they did not know whence the relief came. It pleased him to repair the injustices of fortune, to bring tears of happiness in families pursued by mischance. He was continually plotting, contriving, machinating in the dark, with a childish fear of being caught with his hand in the bag. The greater part of these fine deeds were not known till after his death; the whole of them we shall never know.

"He was a socialist of the right sort! for there are two kinds of them. Those who aspire to appropriate to themselves a part of the goods of others, are numerous and commonplace. To belong to their order it suffices to have a big appetite. Those who are hungering to divide their own goods with men who have none, are rare and precious, for to enter this choice company there is need of a brave and noble heart, free from selfishness, and sensitive to both the happiness and unhappiness of its fellows. Fortunately, the race of these socialists is not extinct, and I feel an unalloyed satisfaction in offering them a tribute they never claim.

"I must be pardoned for dwelling upon this. It does one good to offset the bitterness of so many infamies, so many slanders, so much charlatanism, by resting the eyes upon something more

beautiful, breathing the perfume of these stray corners where simple goodness flowers."

Wagner uses this story of a truly selfless man to remind us that pure generosity and goodness helps to balance the scales of wrongdoing.

"A society in which each member is preoccupied with his own well-being, is organized disorder. This is all that we learn from the irreconcilable conflicts of our uncompromising egoism.

"What does it cost you to speak the truth? Misunderstandings, sometimes sufferings and persecutions. To defend your country? Weariness, wounds and often death. To do good? Annoyance, ingratitude, even resentment. Self-sacrifice enters into all the essential actions of humanity."

Here is a call to action: speak the truth, defend your country, and do good for humanity.

Bridge

I stand on one
Side
Chasm below
Deep and
Dark and
Divisive

Truth is my
Walking stick
I am
Convinced
I carry on my
Back
All the reasons
Why

Pack filled with
The wrongs of
Others
Of needs to be
Met
My map to the
Answers
And I look
Across to
The other
Side

There you
Stand
With your own
Baggage
You have

Innocents to
Protect
And see me
As the
Enemy

Your answers are
Clear to
You
But across the
Fog-filled valley
They are
Hazy to
Me

So I stand
Here
And you stand
There
Unflinching in our
Rightness

The voice
Reaches our
Ears
Let go
See reality
We really know
Nothing
Drop the
Positioning and
Listen

What is there in
Common?
Love
Goodness
Service

Hope
Can we find
The way to
Trust?
Shall we
Build a
Bridge?

Rickety as it
May be
Just start
Somewhere
And let the
Noise of our
Words fall
Away
Leaving only
Footprints

As we
Begin the
Walk to the
Middle
And to each
Other

"The spirit of simplicity is a great magician. It softens asperities, bridges chasms, draws together hands and hearts. The forms which it takes in the world are infinite in number; but never does it seem to us more admirable than when it shows itself across the fatal barriers of position, interest, or prejudice, overcoming the greatest obstacles, permitting those whom everything seems to separate to understand one another, esteem

one another, love one another. This is the true social cement,
that goes into the building of a people."

To endeavor to live simply, love fully, and speak honestly
– while a worthwhile individual ideal – has much farther-
reaching implications. What if we can heal our societal
wounds in the process? Wagner's rich and meaningful
lessons shine even brighter now than when first written.
My hope is that we will take them to heart and that as we
grow towards simplicity individually, we will grow
collectively and experience true and lasting harmony.

A Vital Simplicity Infographic

A Vital Simplicity

practical application of Charles Wagner's insights

Complications

We suffer the consequences of an artificial rather than a natural life.

- Excessive wants
- Preoccupation with the unessential
- Exhibition for the sake of notoriety
- Pride
- Self-centeredness
- Lack of concern for others
- Individual, family, and societal egoism

Solutions

- Work out your mission
- Learn to give
- Recognize the beauty in nature and humanity
- Grow in obedience and humility as your possessions and power increase
- Seek to become better
- Concentrate on the essential
- Balance individual freedom with concern for others
- Teach youth how to entertain themselves
- Encourage children to speak frankly while valuing others' opinions

Simplicity is a state if mind. It dwells in the main intention of our lives.

Promises

- Clarity of purpose
- Joy and liberty
- Confidence and hope
- Recognition of beauty in nature
- Respect given and received
- True connection with others
- Family unity

Societal Unity: The spirit of simplicity is a great magician. It softens roughness, bridges chasms, draws together hands and hearts. The forms which it takes in the world are infinite in number; but never does it seem to us more admirable than when it shows itself across the fatal barriers of position, interest, or prejudice, overcoming the greatest obstacles, permitting those whom everything seems to separate to understand one another, esteem one another, love one another. This is the true social cement that goes into the building of a people.

Bibliography

Bartlett, Monica Y and David DeSteno. "Gratitude and prosocial behavior: helping when it costs you." *PubMed.gov* (2006).

Dauch, Carly, et al. "The influence of the number of toys in the environment on toddlers' play." *Infant Behavior and Development.* (2018).

Iyengar, Sheena and Mark Lepper. "Jam Study." 2000.

Pew Research Center. *About three-in-ten U.S. adults say they are 'almost constantly' online.* Washington, DC: www.pewresearch.org, 2021.

Acknowledgments

Thank you to my sisters, Anita and Karen, who provide incredible encouragement always and gave meaningful suggestions for improving this book.

My group of wise women – Kathy, Carleen, Jo, and Terry – thank you for being a sounding board, reading my manuscript, and providing invaluable input.

Thanks to Malcolm Yarnell for being willing to take time out of your busy schedule to read and comment on this work.

Finally, thank you to my children for reminding me why the simple life matters.

About the Authors

|Suzanne Searcy Johnson|

Suzanne Searcy Johnson is a poet and author drawn to the writings of Charles Wagner. Her simple life is rich with the love of family and friends.

Photo credit: Sarah Gutin Beaty

Also by Suzanne Searcy Johnson
Cherished Clay: a collection of poetry
Forty Lives
Both available on Amazon

suzannesjohnson.com
avitalsimplicity.com

| Charles Wagner |

Charles Wagner (b.1852 d.1918) was a French reformed pastor whose inspirational writings were influential in shaping the reformed theology of his time. His philosophy was  one of Christian love without dogma, espousing a simple life and love of nature. "The Simple Life", written in 1895, was translated into English in 1902.

In 1904, Wagner was invited to preach at the White House by Theodore Roosevelt on whom his book "The Simple Life" had made a lasting impression.

Made in United States
Orlando, FL
23 November 2022

24923320R00098